THE
LANDSCAPE
OF HARMONY

Wendell Berry

Five Seasons Press · 1987

British Library Cataloguing in Publication Data
Berry Wendell
    The landscape of harmony.
    1. Ecology
    I. Title   II Hamburger, Michael
    508   QH541
    ISBN 0 947960 02 3

Printed in England on *one hundred per cent recycled paper*
(see colophon for details)

CONTENTS

PUBLISHER'S NOTE

WENDELL BERRY left his Kentucky farm for a visit to Britain in October 1986. On that occasion he delivered as lectures the two essays published here: PRESERVING WILDNESS was read at the first Temenos Conference at Dartington Hall (October 16th) and DOES COMMUNITY HAVE A VALUE? was given as the seventh Nicholas Bacon Memorial Lecture at the Royal Society of Arts, London (October 19th).

Wendell Berry's last visit had been in 1982, when he and Gary Snyder gave that year's Schumacher Lectures in Bristol. Since then, his books have increasingly attracted attention throughout America whereas in Britain (where he has not been published since Jonathan Cape issued THE BROKEN GROUND in 1966) he remains virtually unknown outside a small but very dedicated readership.

As the intention of this book is to introduce his work to the much larger British audience he deserves, the essays are prefaced by Michael Hamburger's wide-ranging critical assessment of his poetry, fiction and non-fiction. Readers, it is hoped, will be interested to obtain the novels, short stories, poems and essay-collections published in America and now available in Britain. To facilitate ordering from British bookshops, a complete checklist of Wendell Berry's writings is given here, with full details of the trade agents and suppliers.

Special thanks are due to David Bacon who organized the Nicholas Bacon Memorial Lecture and to Kathleen Raine, editor of TEMENOS, who has provided the following account of the first Temenos Conference: *The theme was "Art and the Renewal of the Sacred" and its purpose was to re-affirm the function of the arts as the mirror of the human spirit. On each of the three days of the conference one aspect of humanity's relationship to the sacred was discussed: on the first day, our relationship with the transcendent; on the second, the human field and the arts; on the third, our relationship with 'nature'. Wendell Berry's contribution was made on this third day.*

Glenn Storhaug

A CHECKLIST OF BOOKS BY WENDELL BERRY

(A dash precedes all titles available in Britain in 1987)

FICTION

— NATHAN COULTER, Houghton Mifflin, 1960. Revised and reissued, North Point Press [†], 1985.

— A PLACE ON EARTH, Harcourt Brace, 1967. Revised and reissued, North Point Press [†], 1985.

— THE MEMORY OF OLD JACK, Harcourt Brace Jovanovich, 1974. Harbrace, 1975 (paper). Harvest/HBJ Books [‡], 1986 (rejacketed).

— THE WILD BIRDS, North Point Press [†], 1986. ('Six Stories of the Port William Membership')

POETRY *(some American small press booklets omitted)*

THE BROKEN GROUND, Harcourt Brace, 1964. Jonathan Cape, London, 1966.

OPENINGS, Harcourt Brace, 1986. Harvest Books, 1980 (paper).

FINDINGS, Prairie Press, 1969.

— FARMING: A HANDBOOK, Harcourt Brace Jovanovich, 1970. Harvest Books, 1971 (paper). Harvest/HBJ Books [‡], 1986 (rejacketed).

— THE COUNTRY OF MARRIAGE, Harcourt Brace Jovanovich, 1973. Harvest Books, 1975 (paper). Harvest/HBJ Books [‡], 1986 (rejacketed).

SAYINGS AND DOINGS, Gnomon Press, 1975. (Distributed from the USA by Small Press Distribution Inc, 1814 San Pablo Ave, Berkeley, CA 94702.)

CLEARING, Harcourt Brace Jovanovich, 1977. Harvest Books, 1977 (paper).

— A PART, North Point Press [†], 1980, same, (paper).

— THE WHEEL, North Point Press [†], 1982, same, (paper).

— COLLECTED POEMS 1957-1982, North Point Press [†], 1985.

NON-FICTION

THE LONG-LEGGED HOUSE, Harcourt Brace, 1969. Ballantine, 1971 (paper).

THE HIDDEN WOUND, Houghton Mifflin, 1970. Ballantine, 1971 (paper).

THE UNFORESEEN WILDERNESS, with photographs by Eugene Meatyard, University Press of Kentucky, 1971.

— A CONTINUOUS HARMONY, Harcourt Brace Jovanovich, 1972. Harvest Books, 1975 (paper). Harvest/HBJ Books [‡], 1986 (rejacketed).

— THE UNSETTLING OF AMERICA, Sierra Club Books, 1977. Avon Books 1978 (paper). Reissued by Sierra Club Books (Paperback Library) [§], 1986.

— RECOLLECTED ESSAYS 1965-1980, North Point Press [†], 1981, same, (paper).

— THE GIFT OF GOOD LAND, North Point Press [†], 1981, same, (paper).

— STANDING BY WORDS, North Point Press [†], 1983, same, (paper).
— Editor (with Wes Jackson and Bruce Colman) of MEETING THE EXPECTATIONS OF THE LAND, North Point Press [†], 1985.
— HOME ECONOMICS, North Point Press [†], 1987.

[†] Books published by North Point Press (San Francisco) are distributed in Britain by AIRLIFT BOOK COMPANY, 14 BALTIC STREET, LONDON EC1Y 0TB.

[‡] Books published by Harvest/HBJ (Florida) are distributed in Britain by HBJ LIMITED, FOOTS CRAY, HIGH STREET, SIDCUP, KENT DA14 5HP.

[§] Books published by Sierra Club Books (San Francisco) are distributed in the USA by Random House, warehoused in Europe by EBS, Holland, and are available in Britain through PANDEMIC LIMITED, 71 GREAT RUSSELL STREET, LONDON WC1B 3BN.

THE WRITINGS OF WENDELL BERRY

IT IS IN THE NATURE of Wendell Berry's work to call for very little background information, least of all of a biographical kind. That in his life which is relevant to his writing is also part of it, either explicitly—in poems, novels, stories and essays—or implicitly, because in everything he writes he draws on the totality of his experience, the totality of his vision. It is his distinction to be all of a piece, with the whole man, not only the whole writer, moving at once, together. A central cohesion and wholeness are what his writing is about; and this—in an age when 'things fall apart, the centre cannot hold'—is what makes it different from the work of those specialists in poetry, agriculture, prose fiction, anthropology, sociology, economics or even ecology who do not find it necessary to measure their interests, disciplines or procedures against anything outside or beyond their specializations.

I came to Wendell Berry's work late, in 1975, when a friend at Boston University, where I was a visiting professor, gave me his book of poems THE COUNTRY OF MARRIAGE. Berry's first book of poems, THE BROKEN GROUND, had been published in England in 1966, but I had missed it in my preoccupation with a more peculiarly American kind of poetry that was in the process of breaking through, belatedly also, into

British awareness. Yet THE COUNTRY OF MARRIAGE engaged so directly with other concerns of mine—concerns that had less to do with ways of writing than with ways of living—that I was won over. On a second visit to Boston in 1977 I was able to review his next book of poems, CLEARING, and at least notice the longest and most thoroughly documented of his tracts on culture and agriculture, THE UNSETTLING OF AMERICA. Meanwhile I had begun to search for other books by Wendell Berry, including his novels. The more I have read of his poetry, fiction and essays, the more they have complemented and illuminated one another.

Although Wendell Berry's regional identity, as an American Southerner and Kentucky farmer, is the very base and basis of all his activities—'What I stand for / is what I stand on' is how he puts it in his poem *Below*—and it is far removed from mine, I felt at home immediately in his work. One reason for that has already been touched upon—that Berry's regionalism is not eccentric or centrifugal, but centripetal, and therefore tends towards universality. Another is that, in looking for the roots of his own immediate culture, he has placed himself in a literary tradition not exclusively Southern or even American. Among the twentieth century poets to whom he feels akin are two, W. B. Yeats and Edwin Muir, to whom I owed much in my formative years. Of these two, Edwin Muir is the more unexpected and the more significant affinity, because Muir's poetry has continued to be neglected even in Britain, and that neglect has a bearing on Wendell Berry's practice as a poet. With Edwin Muir he shares a bareness and austerity of utterance that runs counter to almost all the current notions of what makes any one poet's work individual and notable. Richness, complexity and novelty of texture or imagery are among the expected attributes of outstanding poetry. Yet there is a sense in which originality means not novelty or idiosyncrasy, but closeness to the origins of all poetic utterance. It is in this sense that both Edwin Muir's and Wendell Berry's poems are truly and consistently original. Sophistication is what is conspicuously absent from the surface of both poets' verse, though both have wide-ranging and delicately discriminating minds, as their prose works attest. This characteristic of Berry's poems struck me long before I had read his own account of his poetic practice, allegiances and aims in his book of essays STANDING BY WORDS, published in 1983.

In that book Wendell Berry not only defines his position as a poet, but issues a challenge to the specialists—that is, to the majority, as dominant in literature and criticism as in all other fields—quite as radical as his challenge in THE LANDSCAPE OF HARMONY to specialists in social and economic planning; and the two challenges are inseparable, because they spring from a single source. 'The subject of poetry is not words, it is

the world, which poets have in common with other people',
he writes in his essay 'The Specialization of Poetry'; and
again, in his aphoristic 'Notes: Unspecializing Poetry': 'In
contemporary writing about poetry there is little concern for
either workmanship or the truth of poems—in comparison,
say, to the concern for theme, imagery, impact, the psychol-
ogy of "creativity"—because there is so little sense of what, or
whom, the poems are *for*. When we regain a sense of what
poems are for, we will renew the art (the technical means) of
writing them. And so we will renew their ability to tell the
truth.' He goes so far as to deny art that autonomy accorded
to it even by the Marxist poet Brecht, despite Brecht's insist-
ence on the usefulness of poetry, on grounds not the same as
Berry's—though Brecht made a distinction between 'autonomy' and 'autarchy' in the arts. Berry, I am sure, would accept
that distinction, agreeing that poetry must be free to tell its
own truth in its own fashion. What he objects to in much
contemporary poetry and in its critical reception is the autarchy or autocracy of an individualism that has cut itself off
from community; and that is where his aesthetic and poetics
converge with his thinking about culture, agriculture, social
and private life.

As for the modernity that is confused with originality in
our time, his rejection of it also links up with his questioning
of the benefits of more and more technology and automation:

'But what we call the modern world is not necessarily, and not often, the real world, and there is no virtue in being up-to-date in it', he remarks in the context of statements made by other American poets about their work; and more drastically: 'It is a false world, based upon economies and values and desires that are fantastical—a world in which millions of people have lost any idea of the materials, the disciplines, the restraints, and the work necessary to support human life, and have thus become dangerous to their own lives and to the possibility of life.' Because it was in the Romantic period, at the time of the First Industrial Revolution in Europe, that individualism began to hypertrophy to the point of autarchy, Berry's fullest account of the poetic tradition—'Poetry and Place' in the same collection—favours those poets from Dante to Spenser, Shakespeare, Milton and even Dryden and Pope, in whom he finds decorum, good sense, a balance between the values of culture and those of wildness or wilderness—the very subject of his lectures on our own immediate alternatives. In a poem by Shelley, on the other hand, Berry finds a characteristic analogy with the unreal, encapsulated verbiage of present-day technocrats, messages exchanged by expert commentators on the Three Mile Island nuclear accident. 'No high culture without low culture', is the briefest of his epigrams in the book, and Berry's 'motto'. Here 'high' and 'low' must not be understood in terms of class distinctions, but in terms of material needs as against spiritual, intellectual, moral and aesthetic ones. Wendell Berry's constant theme is that the higher and lower activities are interdependent, that our low or material culture must be right if there is to be a higher one at all, because both cultures rest on subsistence and celebration. That is why he can go so far as to assert: 'Perhaps the time has come to say that there is, in reality, no such choice as Yeats's "Perfection of the life, or of the work". The division implied by this proposed choice is not only destructive; it is based upon a shallow understanding of the relation between work and life. The conflicts of life and work, like those of rest and work, would ideally be resolved in balance: *enough* of each. In practice, however, they probably can be resolved (if that is the right word) only in tension, in a principled unwillingness to let go of either, or to sacrifice one to the other. But it is a *necessary* tension, the grief in it both inescapable and necessary.'

The tensions, conflicts and momentary resolutions are enacted in Berry's poems and prose fiction, since both spring with uncommon immediacy from his life as a farmer and university teacher, husband and father, but also always from a sense of a wider community, its way of life and its history. Even the old ways of rural community, with their cooperation in seasonal labour broken only by brief rest or celebration, are not idealized in his imaginative writings, least of all in his early novel NATHAN COULTER. True, even in that novel Berry does not confront the dependence of those ways, in the American South, on the exploitation of Black labourers, a dependence that continued long after the abolition of slavery and the dissolution of the old cotton, rice and tobacco plantations. He made up for that omission in his autobiographical prose piece 'The Hidden Wound', part of which is reprinted in his RECOLLECTED ESSAYS of 1981 as 'Nick and Aunt Georgie'. Though included among his essays, this moving and delicate tribute to two Black workers to whom he was devoted in his childhood would not have been out of place in NATHAN COULTER or his later novels. In NATHAN COULTER, he did confront the violence that could erupt with little provocation in the male characters of three generations, down to the boy protagonist of the novel—a violence due to an imbalance between the high and low cultures even in rural, agrarian communities not wholly disrupted by market forces.

This brings NATHAN COULTER closer than the later novels, A PLACE ON EARTH and THE MEMORY OF OLD JACK, to some of its antecedents in Southern fiction, the peculiar madness and frenzy so prominent in the works of William Faulkner, Carson McCullers or Flannery O'Connor—with due allowances made for differences in the locations of all those works. That seemingly inexplicable, eruptive violence in men otherwise gentle, patient and self-disciplined has historical derivations traced by Berry in his prose piece 'A Native Hill' (now in RECOLLECTED ESSAYS), where he quotes an account of Kentucky road-builders in 1797 who, after strenuous drudgery, suddenly begin to fight among themselves with fire-brands. There he relates the violence in those men to the violence of their task of road-building, itself the assertion of the colonists' urge to eradicate nature, rather than to live in harmony with it.

In the later novels and stories there is more emphasis on the gentleness, patience and orderliness of rural characters still bound to their land by love and care, so that they are sustained inwardly by a reciprocity and continuity that extend beyond their individual lives. Yet in all of them there are characters who do not fit into the pattern, who do not wish to own land or be responsible for its maintenance. These black sheep of the old communities—a line of drunkards or 'loners' stretching from Uncle Burley in NATHAN COULTER (1960) to Uncle Peach in the story 'Thicker than Liquor' in THE WILD BIRDS (1986)—are treated with as much sympathy, understanding and humour as the upholders, like Old Jack Beechum, of the order to which Berry is committed—a vanishing order. Of one of the surviving upholders of that order, Wheeler Catlett in 'Thicker than Liquor', we learn that his need for money 'tended as much towards substantiality as did his love for his bride'; and with that we are back at the heart of Berry's thinking about community and his two cultures, as about the illusory 'materialism' that separates matter from commodity, value from price, and substitutes numerical abstractions for the sustaining realities. From time to time this central concern can become explicit in Berry's fiction and poems, as in the story 'The Wild Birds': 'What he was struggling to make clear is the process by which unbridled economic forces draw life, wealth and intelligence off the farms and out of the country towns and set them in conflict with their sources. Farm produce leaves the farm to enrich an economy that has thrived by the ruin of the land. In this way, in the terms of Wheeler's speech, *price* wars against *value*.'

More often, though, in his novels and stories Berry makes do with what he calls 'the community speech, unconsciously taught and learned, in which words live in the presence of their objects' and which is 'the very root and foundation of language' (STANDING BY WORDS). Since most of his characters are far from being intellectuals, this plain diction is their appropriate medium; but it is also Wendell Berry's preferred diction in his poems. It is in his poetry, therefore, that he takes the greatest risk—not that of being misunderstood, but that of being understood too well and too easily, thus of being rejected both for what he says and for disdaining the ambiguities that would make for a 'suspension of disbelief' in those who do not accept what he is saying.

As in his prose fiction, so in his poetry this plain 'community speech' can convey straight narrative and dialogue, but also an almost mystical undercurrent that allows him to make connections between the concentric orders of human life, like that between love of the land and love between men and women, pervasive not only in THE COUNTRY OF MARRIAGE but in all his imaginative works. So in his story 'The Boundary': 'A shadowless love moves him now, not his, but a love that he belongs to, as he belongs to the place and to the light over it.' For the poetry books, Wendell Berry has resorted to the persona of the 'Mad Farmer' to render some of his more recondite insights, as in *The Mad Farmer in the City*:

Wherever lovely women are the city is undone,
its geometry broken in pieces and lifted,
its streets and corners fading like mist at sunrise
above groves and meadows and planted fields.

In another 'Mad Farmer' poem he admits: 'For I too am perhaps a little mad', and one takes that as being a statement in his own person. Yet it is the Mad Farmer again whose satisfactions include

any man whose words
lead precisely to what exists,
who never stoops to persuasion.

That is why the sober realism of Berry's settings, plots and dialogues very rarely demands direct pointers to the author's own unifying vision and insights, which he has qualified and enlarged from work to work, as once more in THE LAND-SCAPE OF HARMONY, but announced a decade earlier in THE UNSETTLING OF AMERICA: 'The modern urban industrial society is based on a series of radical disconnections between body and soul, husband and wife, marriage and community, community and the earth. At each of these points of discon-nection the collaboration of corporation, government, and experts sets up a profit-making enterprise that results in the further dismemberment and impoverishment of the Crea-tion.' The rural characters in his fiction do not talk in those terms; but they embody the alternative to the same discon-nection by what they are and do, as in the rhythm of labour and rest, subsistence and celebration, that is also essential to much of Berry's poetry:

> One thing work gives
> is the joy of not working,
> a minute here or there
> when I stand and only breathe
> receiving the good of the air.

Wendell Berry would be a lesser poet if behind his plain words and plain statements like this one there did not lie 'heart mysteries', as Yeats called them, as well as tensions and paradoxes that the most 'ordinary' of men and women can ex-perience, without being able to put them into words like 'The light that is mine is not / mine' or 'When the mind's an empty room/The clear days come' (THE COUNTRY OF MARRIAGE). This is the transparent simplicity at which Berry excels.

To those who accept Wendell Berry's basic connections, because they know and recognize them from their own needs and conflicts, he seems 'a little mad' only in the persistence and consistency with which he has applied himself to resisting the dominant, established insanities of our age. Such whole-heartedness and single-mindedness have become so rare as to look eccentric now, when in fact they are the attributes of a securely centred, integrated awareness. That Berry's is also a self-critical one, open to correction (like his works) and scrupulous in its weighing up of interests and views opposed to his own, will be apparent to readers of his lectures, as of THE UNSETTLING OF AMERICA or its sequel THE GIFT OF GOOD LAND.

To trace the subtle modulations of manner and substance in his successive works would demand more space than I can decently take up here. Nor can I indicate the range of his poetry from elegy to song, from narrative to epigram, from historical commemoration to reflections on topical issues like the Vietnam War. Most of his poetry has been gathered into the COLLECTED POEMS 1957–1982; and most of his major prose writings are also available from North Point Press, San Francisco. If I have refrained from trying very hard to place

Wendell Berry as a poet, novelist or defender of community values, it is because he has made the necessary acknowledgements to predecessors and to associates like Gary Snyder—one of the poets, incidentally, who preoccupied me in the Sixties, and one who has arrived at a position close to Berry's by a very different route, initiation into Zen Buddhism and an immersion in the most various cultural and religious traditions. That two remarkable poets so little alike in their starting-points and their ways could meet on common, central, ground, bears out what I said about the centrality and universality of Berry's concerns.

Until recently, in Britain the antagonism between urban industrial society and nature as wilderness or wildness was not nearly as acute as in America, both because by far the greater part of the country has been cultivated for so long that most of its natural history has been conditioned by its political, social and economic history, and because few British people had lost contact with nature to the same degree as many urban Americans. In Britain, too, as in Europe and everywhere, the balance between the two orders—between the autonomy of technical or commercial enterprise and the needs of communities—has become precarious to the point of crisis, so much so as to threaten the future not only of residual wildness but of agriculture. (I write this in a part of Suffolk where tap water has to be filtered for drinking or boiling, because of the seepage of chemicals from the farms, and where a second, controversial type of, nuclear power station is planned on what is still designated as our 'heritage coast', while most of the older industries, crafts and skills of the region have been driven into obsolescence.) I can be no more sure about the potential effectiveness of Wendell Berry's writings in Britain than about their effectiveness in his own country, but I have no doubts about their potential appeal. For one thing, his imaginative work is truly conservative, in a sense belied by the political parties on both sides of the ocean that lay claim to that name; and it is also radical, in the sense of going to the roots, not in the equally misleading sense that makes it synonymous with 'extremist' or 'fanatical'. (The root of a tree is one of its extremities, but it is also that part which nourishes and stabilizes all its growth.) For another, Berry's plainness and directness of language in the imaginative works keep them free from the divisive jargon of trends, 'camps' and fashions, so that they are accessible to anyone who cares for the essential, substantial words. As for his testimony in the lectures, it is as urgent as it is balanced and reasoned. Even on that level of discourse, different in kind as it had to be from that of the fiction and poems, Berry's rare sanity and wisdom find their right tone, at once eloquent with conviction and supple enough to respond to the doubts of the unconvinced.

The Landscape of Harmony

Preserving Wildness

PRESERVING WILDNESS

THE ARGUMENT over the proper relation of humanity to nature is becoming, as the Sixties used to say, polarized. The result, as before, is bad talk on both sides. At one extreme are those who sound as if they are entirely in favour of nature; they assume that there is no necessary disjuncture or difference between the human estate and the estate of nature, that human good is in some simple way the same as natural good. They believe, at least in principle, that the biosphere is an egalitarian system, in which all creatures, including humans, are equal in value and have an equal right to live and flourish. These people tend to stand aloof from the issue of the proper human use of nature. Indeed, they have begun to use 'stewardship' (meaning the responsible use of nature) as a term of denigration.

At the other extreme are the nature conquerors, who have no patience with an old-fashioned outdoor farm, let alone a wilderness. These people divide all reality into two parts: human good, which they define as profit, comfort, and security; and everything else, which they understand as a stockpile of 'natural resources' or 'raw materials', which will sooner or later be transformed into human good. The aims of these militant tinkerers invariably manage to be at once unimpeachable and suspect. They wish earnestly, for example, to solve what they call 'the problem of hunger'—if it can be done glamorously, comfortably, and profitably. They believe that the ability to do something is the reason to do it. According to a recent press release from the University of Illinois College of Agriculture, researchers there are looking forward to 'food production without either farmers or farms'. (This is perhaps the first explicit acknowledgement of the programme that has been implicit in the work of the land-grant universities for forty or fifty years.)

If I had to choose, I would join the nature extremists against the technology extremists, but this choice seems poor, even assuming that it is possible. I would prefer to stay in the middle, not to avoid taking sides, but because I think the middle *is* a side, as well as the real location of the problem.

The middle, of course, is always rather roomy and bewildering territory, and so I should state plainly the assumptions that define the ground on which I intend to stand:

1. We live in a wilderness, in which we and our works occupy a tiny space and play a tiny part. We exist under its dispensation and by its tolerance.

2. This wilderness, the universe, is *somewhat* hospitable to us, but it is also absolutely dangerous to us (it is going to kill us, sooner or later), and we are absolutely dependent upon it.

3. That we depend upon what we are endangered by is a problem not solvable by 'problem solving'. It does not have what the nature romantic or the technocrat would regard as a solution. We are not going back to the Garden of Eden, nor are we going to manufacture an Industrial Paradise.

4. There does exist a possibility that we can live more or less in harmony with our native wilderness; I am betting my life that such a harmony is possible. But I do not believe that it can be achieved simply or easily or that it can ever be perfect, and I am certain that it can never be made once for all, but is the forever unfinished lifework of our species.

5. It is not possible (at least, not for very long) for humans to intend their own good specifically or exclusively. We cannot intend our good, in the long run, without intending the good of our place—which means, ultimately, the good of the world.

6. To use or not to use nature is not a choice that is available to us; we can live only at the expense of other lives. Our choice has rather to do with how and how much to use. This is not a choice that can be decided satisfactorily in principle or in theory; it is a choice intransigently practical. That is, it must be worked out in local practice because, by necessity, the practice will vary somewhat from one locality to another. There is, thus, no *practical* way that we can intend the good of the world. Practice can only be local.

7. If there is no escape from the human use of nature, then human good cannot be simply synonymous with natural good.

What these assumptions describe, of course, is the human predicament. It is a spiritual predicament, for it requires us to be properly humble and grateful; time and again, it asks us to be still and wait. But it is also a practical problem, for it requires us to *do* things.

In going to work on this problem it is a mistake to proceed on the basis of an assumed division or divisibility between nature and humanity, or wildness and domesticity, but it is also a mistake to assume that there is no difference. If these things could be divided, our life would be far simpler and easier than it is, just as it would be if they were not different. Our problem, exactly, is that the human and the natural are indivisible, and yet are different.

The indivisibility of wildness and domesticity, even within the fabric of human life itself, is easy enough to demonstrate. Our bodily life, to begin at the nearest place, is half wild. Perhaps it is more than half wild, for it is dependent upon reflexes, instincts, and appetites that we do not cause or intend and that we cannot, or had better not, stop. We live, partly, because we are domestic creatures—that is, we participate in our human economy to the extent that we 'make a living'; we are able, with variable success, to discipline our appetites and instincts in order to produce this artifact, this human living. And yet it is equally true that we breathe and our hearts beat and we survive as a species because we are wild.

The same is true of a healthy human economy as it branches upward out of the soil. The topsoil, to the extent that it is fertile, is wild; it is a dark wilderness, ultimately unknowable, teeming with wildlife. A forest or a crop, no matter how intentionally husbanded by human foresters or farmers, will be found to be healthy precisely to the extent that it is wild—able to collaborate with earth, air, light and water in the way common to plants before humans walked the earth. We know from experience that we can increase our domestic demands upon plants so far that we force them into kinds of failure that wild plants do not experience.

Breeders of domestic animals, likewise, know that, when a breeding programme is too much governed by human intention, by economic considerations, or by fashion, uselessness is the result. Size or productivity, for instance, will be gained at the cost of health, vigour, or reproductive ability. In other words, so-called domestic animals must remain half wild, or more than half, because they are creatures of nature. Humans are intelligent enough to select for a type of creature; they are not intelligent enough to *make* a creature. Their efforts to make an entirely domestic animal, like their efforts to make an entirely domestic human, are doomed to failure because they do not have and undoubtedly are never going to have the full set of production standards for the making of creatures. From a human point of view, then, creature making is wild. The effort to make plants, animals, and humans ever more governable by human intentions is continuing with more determination and more violence than ever, but that does not mean that it is nearer to success. It means only that we are increasing the violence and the magnitude of the expectable reactions.

To be divided against nature, against wildness, then, is a human disaster because it is to be divided against ourselves. It confines our identity as creatures entirely within the bounds of our own understanding, which is invariably a mistake because it is invariably reductive. It reduces our largeness, our mystery, to a petty and sickly comprehensibility.

But to say that we are not divided and not dividable from nature is not to say that there is no difference between us and the other creatures. Human nature partakes of nature, participates in it, and yet is different from it. We feel the difference as discomfort or difficulty or danger. Nature is not easy to live with. It is hard to have rain on your cut hay, or floodwater over your cropland, or coyotes in your sheep; it is hard when nature does not respect your intentions, and she never does exactly respect them. Moreover, such problems belong to all of us, to the human lot. Humans who do not experience them are exempt only because they are paying (or underpaying) other humans such as farmers to deal with nature on their behalf. Further, it is not just agriculture-dependent humanity that has had to put up with natural dangers and frustrations; these have been the lot of hunting and gathering societies also, and the wild creatures do not always live comfortably or easily with nature either.

But humans differ most from other creatures in the extent to which they must be *made* what they are—that is, in the extent to which they are artifacts of their culture. It is true that what we might as well call culture does go into the making of some birds and animals, but this teaching is so much less than the teaching that makes a human as to be almost a different thing. To take a creature who is biologically a human and to make him or her fully human is a task that requires many years (some of us sometimes fear that it requires more than a lifetime), and this long effort of human making is necessary, I think, because of our power. In the hierarchy of power among the earth's creatures, we are at the top, and we have been growing stronger for a long time. We are now, to ourselves, incomprehensibly powerful, capable of doing more damage than floods, storms, volcanoes, and earthquakes. And so it is more important than ever that we should have cultures capable of prudence, justice, fortitude, temperance, and the other virtues. For our history reveals that, stripped of the restraints, disciplines, and ameliorations of culture, humans are not 'natural', not 'thinking animals' or 'naked apes', but monsters—indiscriminate and insatiable killers and destroyers. We differ from other creatures, partly, in our susceptibility to monstrosity. It is perhaps for this reason that, in the wake of the great wars of our century, we have seen poets such as T. S. Eliot, Ezra Pound, and David Jones making an effort to reweave the tattered garment of culture and to reestablish the cultural tasks, which are, as Pound put it, 'To know the histories / to know good from evil / And know whom to trust.' And we see, if we follow Pound a little further, that the recovery of culture involves, leads to, or is the recovery of nature:

> the trees rise
> and there is a wide sward between them
> . . . myrrh and olibanum on the altar stone
> giving perfume,
>   and where was nothing
> now is furry assemblage
>   and in the boughs now are voices . . .

In the recovery of culture *and* nature is the knowledge of how to farm well, how to preserve, harvest, and replenish the forests, how to make, build, and use, return and restore. In this *double* recovery, which is the recovery of our humanity, is the hope that the domestic and the wild can exist together in lasting harmony.

This doubleness of allegiance and responsibility, difficult as it always is, confusing as it sometimes is, apparently is inescapable. A culture that does not measure itself by nature, by an understanding of its debts to nature, becomes destructive of nature and thus of itself. A culture that does not measure itself by its own best work and the best work of other cultures (the determination of which is its unending task) becomes destructive of itself and thus of nature.

Harmony is one phase, the good phase, of the inescapable dialogue between culture and nature. In this phase, humans consciously and conscientiously ask of their work: Is this good for us? Is this good for our place? And the questioning and answering in this phase is minutely particular: It can occur only with reference to particular artifacts, events, places, ecosystems, and neighbourhoods. When the cultural side of the dialogue becomes too theoretical or abstract, the other phase, the bad one, begins. Then the conscious, responsible questions are not asked; acts begin to be committed and things to be made on their own terms for their own sakes, culture deteriorates, and nature retaliates.

The awareness that we are slowly growing into now is that the earthly wildness that we are so complexly dependent upon is at our mercy. It has become, in a sense, our artifact because it can only survive by a human understanding and forbearance that we now must make. The only thing we have to preserve nature with is culture; the only thing we have to preserve wildness with is domesticity.

To me, this means simply that we are not safe in assuming that we can perserve wildness by making wilderness preserves. Those of us who see that wildness and wilderness need to be preserved are going to have to understand the dependence of these things upon our domestic economy and our domestic behaviour. If we do not have an economy capable of valuing in particular terms the durable good of localities and communities, then we are not going to be able to preserve anything. We are going to have to see that, if we want our forests to last, then we must make wood products that last, for our forests are more threatened by shoddy workmanship than by clear-cutting or by fire. Good workmanship—that is, careful, considerate, and loving work—requires us to think considerately of the whole process, natural and cultural, involved in the making of wooden artifacts, because the good worker does not share the industrial contempt for 'raw material'. The good worker loves the board before it becomes a table, loves the tree before it yields the board, loves the forest before it gives up the tree. The good worker understands that a badly made artifact is both an insult to its user and a danger to its source. We could say, then, that good forestry begins with the respectful husbanding of the forest that we call stewardship and ends with well-made tables and chairs and houses, just as good agriculture begins with stewardship of the fields and ends with good meals.

In other words, conservation is going to prove increasingly futile and increasingly meaningless if its proscriptions are not answered positively by an economy that rewards and enforces good use. I would call this a loving economy, for it would strive to place a proper value on all the materials of the world, in all their metamorphoses from soil and water, air and light to the finished goods of our towns and households, and I think that the only effective motive for this would be a particularizing love for local things, rising out of local knowledge and local allegiance.

Our present economy, by contrast, does not account for affection at all, which is to say that it does not account for value. It is simply a description of the career of money as it preys upon both nature and human society. Apparently because our age is so manifestly unconcerned for the life of the spirit, many people conclude that it places an undue value on

material things. But that cannot be so, for people who valued
material things would take care of them and would care for
the sources of them. We could argue that an age that *properly*
valued and cared for material things would be an age properly spiritual. In my part of the United States, the Shakers,
'unworldly' as they were, were the true materialists, for they
truly valued materials. And they valued them in the only way
that such things *can* be valued in practice: by good workmanship, both elegant and sound. The so-called materialism of
our own time is, by contrast, at once indifferent to spiritual
concerns and insatiably destructive of the material world.
And I would call our economy, not materialistic, but abstract,
intent upon the subversion of both spirit and matter by abstractions of value and of power. In such an economy, it is
impossible to value anything that one *has*. What one has
(house or job, spouse or car) is only valuable insofar as it can
be exchanged for what one believes that one wants—a limit-
less economic process based upon boundless dissatisfaction.

Now that the practical processes of industrial civilization
have become so threatening to humanity and to nature, it is
easy for us, or for some of us, to see that practicality needs to
be made subject to spiritual values and spiritual measures.
But we must not forget that it is also necessary for spirituality
to be responsive to practical questions. For human beings the
spiritual and the practical are, and should be, inseparable.

Alone, practicality becomes dangerous; spirituality, alone, becomes feeble and pointless. Alone, either becomes dull. Each is the other's discipline, in a sense, and in good work the two are joined.

'The dignity of toil is undermined when its necessity is gone', Kathleen Raine says, and she is right. It is an insight that we dare not ignore, and I would emphasize that it applies to *all* toil. What is not needed is frivolous. Everything depends on our right relation to necessity—and therefore on our right definition of necessity. In defining our necessity, we must be careful to discount the subsidies, the unrepaid borrowings, from nature that have so far sustained industrial civilization: the 'cheap' fossil fuels and ores; the forests that have been cut down and not replanted; the virgin soils of much of the world, whose fertility has not been replenished.

And so, though I am trying to unspecialize the idea and the job of preserving wildness, I am not against wilderness preservation. I am only pointing out, as the Reagan administration has done, that the wildernesses we are trying to preserve are standing squarely in the way of our present economy, and that the wildernesses cannot survive if our economy does not change.

The reason to preserve wilderness is that we need it. We need wilderness of all kinds, large and small, public and private. We need to go now and again into places where our work is disallowed, where our hopes and plans have no standing. We need to come into the presence of the unqualified and mysterious formality of Creation. And I would agree with Edward Abbey that we need as well some tracts of what he calls 'absolute wilderness' which 'through general agreement none of us enters at all'.

We need wilderness also because wildness—nature—is one of our indispensable studies. We need to understand it as our source and preserver, as an essential measure of our history and behaviour, and as the ultimate definer of our possibilities. There are, I think, three questions that must be asked with respect to a human economy in any given place:

1. What is here?
2. What will nature permit us to do here?
3. What will nature help us to do here?

The second and third questions are obviously the ones that would define agendas of practical research and of work. If we do not work with and within natural tolerances, then we will not be permitted to work for long. It is plain enough, for example, that if we use soil fertility faster than nature can replenish it, we are proposing an end that we do not desire. And to ignore the possibility of help from nature makes farming, for example, too expensive for farmers—as we are seeing. It may make life too expensive for humans.

But the second and third questions are ruled by the first. They cannot be answered—they cannot intelligently be asked—until the first has been answered. And yet the first question has not been answered, or asked, so far as I know, in the whole history of the American economy. All the great changes, from the Indian wars and the opening of agricultural frontiers to the inauguration of genetic engineering, have been made without a backward look and in ignorance of whereabouts. Our response to the forest and the prairie that covered our present fields was to get them out of the way as soon as possible. And the obstructive human populations of Indians and 'inefficient' or small farmers have been dealt with in the same spirit. We have never known what we were doing because we have never known what we were *un*doing. We cannot know what we are doing until we know what nature would be doing if we were doing nothing. And that is why we need small native wildernesses widely dispersed over the countryside as well as large ones in spectacular places.

However, to say that wilderness and wildness are indispensable to us, indivisible from us, is not to say that we can find sufficient standards for our life and work in nature. To suggest that, for humans, there is a simple equation between 'natural' and 'good' is to fall prey immediately to the cynics who love to point out that, after all, 'everything is natural'.

They are, of course, correct. Nature provides bountifully for her children, but, as we would now say, she is also extremely permissive. If her children want to destroy one another entirely or to commit suicide, that is all right with her. There is nothing, after all, more natural than the extinction of species; the extinction of *all* species, we must assume, would also be perfectly natural.

Clearly, if we want to argue for the existence of the world as we know it, we will have to find some way of qualifying and supplementing this relentless criterion of 'natural'. Perhaps we can do so only by a reaffirmation of a lesser kind of naturalness—that of self-interest. Certainly human self-interest has much wickedness to answer for, and we are living in just fear of it; nevertheless, we must take care not to condemn it absolutely. After all, we value this passing work of nature that we call 'the natural world', with its graceful plenty of animals and plants, precisely because *we* need it and love it and want it for a home.

We are creatures obviously subordinate to nature, dependent upon a wild world that we did not make. And yet we are joined to that larger nature by our own nature, a part of which is our self-interest. A common complaint nowadays is that humans think the world is 'anthropocentric', or human-centred. I understand the complaint; the assumptions of so-called anthropocentrism often result in gross and dangerous insubordination. And yet I don't know how the human species can avoid some version of self-centredness; I don't know how any species can. An earthworm, I think, is living in an earthworm-centred world; the thrush who eats the earthworm is living in a thrush-centred world; the hawk who eats the thrush is living in a hawk-centred world. Each creature, that is, does what is necessary in its own behalf, and is domestic in its own *domus* or home.

Humans differ from earthworms, thrushes and hawks in their capacity to do more—in modern times a great deal more—in their own behalf than is necessary. Moreover, the vast majority of humans in the industrial nations are guilty of this extravagence. One of the oldest human arguments is over the question of how much is necessary. How much must humans do in their own behalf in order to be fully human? The number and variety of the answers ought to notify us that we never have known for sure, and yet we have the disquieting suspicion that, almost always, the honest answer has been 'less'.

We have no way to work at this question, it seems to me, except by perceiving that, in order to have the world, we must share it, both with each other and with other creatures, which is immediately complicated by the further perception that, in order to live in the world, we must use it somewhat at the expense of other creatures. We must acknowledge both the centrality and the limits of our self-interest. One can hardly imagine a tougher situation.

But in the recognition of the difficulty of our situation is a kind of relief, for it makes us give up the hope that a a solution can be found in a simple preference for humanity over nature or nature over humanity. The only solutions we have ahead of us will need to be worked for and worked out. They will have to be practical solutions, resulting in good local practice. There is work to do that can be done.

As we undertake this work, perhaps the greatest immediate danger lies in our dislike of ourselves as a species. This is an understandable dislike—we are justly afraid of ourselves— but we are nevertheless obliged to think and act out of a proper self-interest and a genuine self-respect as human beings. Otherwise, we will allow our dislike and fear of ourselves to justify further abuses of one another and the world. We must come to terms with the fact that it is not natural to be disloyal to one's own kind.

For these reasons, there is great danger in the perception that 'there are too many people', whatever truth may be in it, for this is a premise from which it is too likely that somebody, sooner or later, will proceed to a determination of *who* are the surplus. If we conclude that there are too many, it is hard to avoid the further conclusion that there are some we do not need. But how many do we need, and which ones? Which ones, now apparently unnecessary, may turn out later to be indispensable? We do not know; it is part of our mystery, our wildness, that we do not know.

I would argue that, at least for us in the United States, the conclusion that 'there are too many people' is premature, not because I know that there are *not* too many people, but because I do not think we are prepared to come to such a conclusion. I grant that questions about population size need to be asked, but they are not the *first* questions that need to be asked.

The 'population problem', initially, should be examined as a problem, not of quantity, but of pattern. Before we conclude that we have too many people, we must ask if we have people who are misused, people who are misplaced, or people who are abusing the places they have. The facts of most immediate importance may be, not how many we are, but where we are and what we are doing. At any rate, the attempt to solve our problems by reducing our numbers may be a distraction from the overriding population statistic of our time: that *one* human with a nuclear bomb and the will to use it is 100 per cent too many. I would argue that it is not human fecundity that is overcrowding the world so much as technological multipliers of the power of individual humans. The worst disease of the world now is probably the ideology of technological heroism, according to which more and more people willingly cause large-scale effects that they do not foresee and that they cannot control. This is the ideology of the professional class of the industrial nations—a class whose allegiance to communities and places has been dissolved by their economic motives and by their educations. These are people who will go anywhere and jeopardize anything in order to assure the success of their careers.

We may or may not have room for more people, but it is certain that we do not have room for more technological heroics. We do not need any more thousand-dollar solutions to ten-dollar problems or million-dollar solutions to thousand-dollar problems—or multi-billion dollar solutions where there was never a problem at all. We have no way to compute the inhabitability of our places; we cannot weigh or measure the pleasures we take in them; we cannot say how many dollars domestic tranquillity is worth. And yet we must now learn to bear in mind the memory of communities destroyed, disfigured, or made desolate by technological events, as well as the memory of families dispossessed, displaced, and impoverished by 'labour-saving' machines. The issue of human obsolescence may be more urgent for us now than the issue of human population.

The population issue thus leads directly to the issue of

proportion and scale. What is the proper amount of power for a human to use? What are the proper limits of human enterprise? How may these proprieties be determined? Such questions may seem inordinately difficult, but that is because we have gone too long without asking them. One of the fundamental assumptions of industrial economics has been that such questions are outmoded and that we need never ask them again. The failure of that assumption now requires us to reconsider the claims of wildness and to renew our understanding of the old ideas of propriety and harmony.

When we propose that humans should learn to behave properly with respect to nature so as to place their domestic economy harmoniously upon and within the sustaining and surrounding wilderness, then we make possible a sort of landscape criticism. Then we can see that it is not primarily the number of people inhabiting a landscape that determines the propriety of the ratio and the relation between human domesticity and wildness, but it is the way people divide the landscape and use it. We can see that it is the landscape of monoculture in which both nature and humanity are most at risk. We feel the human fragility of the huge one-class housing development, just as we feel the natural fragility of the huge one-crop field.

Looking at the monocultures of industrial civilization, we yearn with a kind of homesickness for the humanness and the naturalness of a highly diversified, multipurpose landscape, democratically divided, with many margins. The margins are of the utmost importance. They are the divisions between holdings, as well as between kinds of work and kinds of land. These margins—lanes, streamsides, wooden fencerows, and the like—are always freeholds of wildness, where limits are set on human intention. Such places are hospitable to the wild lives of plants and animals and to the wild play of human children. They enact, within the bounds of human domesticity itself, a human courtesy toward the wild that is one of the best safeguards of designated tracts of true wilderness. This is the landscape of harmony, safer far for life of all kinds than the landscape of monoculture. And we should not neglect to notice that, whereas the monocultural landscape is totalitarian in tendency, the landscape of harmony is democratic and free.

Does Community Have a Value?

DOES COMMUNITY HAVE A VALUE?

COMMUNITY IS A CONCEPT, like humanity or peace, that virtually no one has taken the trouble to quarrel with; even its worst enemies praise it. There is almost no product or project that is not being advocated in the name of community improvement. We are told that we, as a community, are better off for the power industry, the defence industry, the communications industry, the transportation industry, the agriculture industry, the food industry, the health industry, the medical industry, the insurance industry, the sports industry, the beauty industry, the entertainment industry, the mining industry, the education industry, the law industry, the government industry, and the religion industry. You could look into any one of those industries and find many people, some of them in influential positions, who are certifiably 'community spirited'.

In fact, however, neither our economy, nor our government, nor our educational system runs on the assumption that community has a value—a value, that is, that *counts* in any practical or powerful way. The values that are assigned to community are emotional and spiritual—'cultural'—which makes it the subject of pieties that are merely vocal. But does community have a value that is practical or economic?

Is community necessary? If it does not have a value that is practical and economic, if it is not necessary, then *can* it have a value that is emotional and spiritual? Can 'community values' be preserved simply for their own sake? Can people be neighbours, for example, if they do not need each other or help each other? Can there be a harvest festival where there is no harvest? Does economy have spiritual value?

Such questions are being forced upon us now by the loss of community. We are discouraged from dealing with them by their difficulty in such a time as this, and yet these questions and others like them are indispensable to us, for they describe the work that we must do. We can only be encouraged to see that this work, though difficult, is fascinating and hopeful. It is homework, doable in some part by everybody, useful to everybody—as far as possible unlike the massive, expensive, elitist projects that now engross virtually every government of the world.

But before I go any farther, let me make clear what I mean by community. I will give as particular an example as I know.

My friends Loyce and Owen Flood married in October, 1938, and moved to a farm in hilly country near Port Royal, Kentucky. She was seventeen; Owen was eighteen.

Loyce had graduated from high school and had been to college for a short while. Although she had been raised on a farm she did not know a great deal about being a farmer's wife on a small, poor hillside place. She and Owen had little money, and she had to learn quickly the arts of subsistence.

Fortunately, they were living in a neighbourhood of households closely bound together by family ties or friendships and by well-established patterns of work and pleasure. This neighbourhood included, in varying degrees of intimacy and interdependency, nine households, all more or less within walking distance. The women kept house individually, but all the big jobs they did together: housecleaning, wall papering, quilting, canning, cooking for field crews. Though Loyce looked up to them and called them 'Miss Suzy', 'Miss Berthy', and so on, most of them were still fairly young, in their late thirties or early forties. They were a set of hearty, humorous, industrious women, who saw whatever was funny and loved to make up funny names for things.

They became Loyce's teachers, and now, nearly fifty years later, she remembers with warmth and pleasure their kindness to her and their care for her. They helped her to learn to cook and can, to work in the hog killing and in the field (for at planting and harvest times, the women went to the field with the men); they looked after her when she was sick; they taught her practical things, and things having to do with their mutual womanhood and community life. Although she had more formal schooling than any of them, she says now,

'Everything I know I learned from those people.' And the men were as kind and useful to Owen as the women were to Loyce. 'They took us under their wing,' she says.

The men farmed their own farms, but, like the women, they did the big jobs together. And when they worked together, they ate together. They always had a big dinner. 'They never shirked dinner,' Loyce says, 'that was one thing sure.' In hot weather, chicken would be the only fresh meat available, and they ate a lot of chicken. The women were perfectionists at making noodles.

By our standards now, these people were poor. The farms ranged in size from thirty-seven to perhaps a hundred acres. But only the thirty-seven acre farm was entirely tillable. The others included a lot of 'hill and holler'. Then, as now, most of the money made on the produce of that place was made by manufacturers and merchants in other places; probably no household grossed more than $1,000 a year. And so the subsistence economy was necessarily elaborate and strong. The people raised and slaughtered their own meat, raised vegetable gardens, produced their own milk, butter, and eggs. They gathered the wild fruit as it ripened. They canned and dried and cured and preserved. They spent little money. The cash from the household came mainly from the sale of cream, and each farm kept three or four milk cows for that purpose. Loyce remembers that her weekly cream cheque was three dollars; they budgeted half of that for groceries and gasoline for the car and half for payment on a debt.

These people worked hard, and without any modern labour savers. They had no tractors, no electricity, no refrigerators, no washing machines, no vacuum cleaners. Their one luxury was the telephone party line, which cost fifty cents a month. But their work was in limited quantities; they did not work at night or away from home; they knew their work, they knew how to work, and they knew each other. Loyce says, 'They didn't have to do a lot of explaining.'

Their work was mingled with their amusement; sometimes it *was* their amusement. Talk was very important. They worked together and talked; they saw each other in Port Royal on Saturday night and talked; on Sunday morning they went to church early and stood around outside and talked; when church was over, they talked and were in no hurry to go home.

In the summer they would get fifty pounds of ice and make ice cream, and eat the whole freezer full, and sometimes make another, and eat that. In the winter they would all go to somebody's house at night and pop corn, and the men would play cards and the women would talk. They played cards a lot. One of the households had books that could be borrowed. Loyce's private amusements were reading and embroidery. She does not remember ever getting lonesome or bored.

There are, as I see it, two salient facts about this neighbour-hood of 1938:

1. It was effective and successful as a community. It did what we know that a good community does: it supported itself, amused itself, consoled itself, and passed its knowledge on to the young. It was something to build on.

2. It no longer exists. By the end of World War II, it was both reduced and altered, and the remnants of its old life are now mainly memories.

The reasons why it no longer exists are numerous and com-plexly interrelated. Some of them are: increased farm income during and after the war; improved roads and vehicles; the influence of radio and then of television; rising economic ex-pectations; changing social fashions; school consolidation; and the rapid introduction of industrial technology into agriculture after the war. Thus, the disappearance of this community into the modern world and the industrial economy is both a fact, and to a considerable extent an un-derstandable fact.

But we must take care not to stop with the mere recog-nition and understanding of facts. We must go ahead to ask if the fact exists for our good, if it can be understood to our good, and if its existence is necessary or inescapable. After establishing that a community has died, for example, we must ask who has been served by its death.

Such a community as I have described has often been caricatured and ridiculed and often sentimentalized. But, looked at in its facts, as my friend recalls them, it escapes both extremes. The people were manifestly equal to their lot; they were not oafish or stupid. On the other hand, they were not perfect; they were not living an idyll. The community was not immune either to change or to the need to change. Anyone familiar with the history of farming on Kentucky hillsides knows that its practices could always have been improved.

But another fact that we must now reckon with is that this community did not change by improving itself. It changed by turning away from itself, from its place, from its own possibility. Somehow the periphery exhausted and broke the centre. This community, like thousands of similar ones, was not changed by anything that *it* thought of, nor by anything thought of by anybody who believed that community had a practical or an economic value. It was changed, partly to its own blame, by forces, originating outside itself, that did not consider, much less desire, the welfare or the existence of such communities. This community, like any other, had to change and needed to change, but what if its own life, its own good, had been the standard by which it changed, rather than the profit of distant entrepreneurs and corporations?

We are left with questions—that one and others.

Is such a community desirable? My answer, unhesitatingly, is yes. But that is an answer notoriously subject to the charge of sentimentality or nostalgia. People will ask if I 'want to turn back the clock'. And so I am pushed along to another question, a more interesting one: Is such a community necessary? Again, I think, the answer must be yes, and here we have access to some manner of proof.

For one thing, the place once occupied by that community is now occupied by people who are not, in the same close, effective sense, a community. The place is no longer central to its own interest and its own economy. The people do not support themslves so much from the place or so much by mutual work and help as their predecessors did; they furnish much less of their own amusement and consolation; purchasing has more and more replaced growing and making; and less and less of local knowledge and practical skill is passed on to the young. In 1938, the community and its economy were almost identical. Today, the community is defined mostly by the mere proximity of its people to one another. The people belong, often to their own detriment, to a *national* economy whose centres are far from home.

For another thing, we now have before us the failure of the industrial system of agriculture that supplanted the community and the ways of 1938. There is, so far as I am aware, no way of denying the failure of an agricultural system that destroys both land and people, as the industrial system is now doing. Obviously, we need a way of farming that attaches people to the land much more intimately, carefully, and democratically than the industrial system has been able to do, and we can neither establish good farming nor preserve it without successful communities.

It is easy to suppose, as many powerful people apparently have done, that the principle of subsistence on family farms and in rural communities will be bad for the larger economy, but this supposition has proved to be a dangerous and destructive error. Subsistence is bad for the industrial economy and for the paper economy of the financiers; it is good for the actual, real-world economy by which people live and are fed, clothed, and housed. For example, in 1938, in the time of subsistence, there were three thriving grocery stores that were patronized by the neighbourhood I have been talking about—one at Drennon's Lick and two at Port Royal. Now there is only one, at Port Royal. The 'standard of living' (determined, evidently, by how much money is spent) has increased, but community life has declined, economically and every other way. In the neighbourhoods around Port Royal, we now have many labour-saving devices, but we buy and pay for them farther and farther from home. And we have fewer and fewer people at home who know how to maintain these devices and keep them running. Port Royal, in other words, now exists for 'the economy'—that abstract accumulation of monetary power which aggrandizes corporations and governments and which does not concern itself at all for the existence of Port Royal.

For many years, I think, the people of rural America have been struggling with the realization that we are living in a colony. It is an irony especially bitter for Americans that, having cast off the colonialism of England, we have proceeded to impose a domestic colonialism on our own land and people, and yet we cannot deny that most of the money made on the products that we produce in rural America—food and fibre, timber, mineable fuels and minerals of all kinds—is made by other people in other places. We cannot deny that all of these fundamental enterprises, as now conducted, involve the destruction of the land and the people. We cannot deny that there is no provision being made and no thought being taken in any segment of the rural economy for the long-term welfare of the people who are doing the work. Indeed, we cannot deny that our leaders appear to take for granted that the eventual destruction of lives, livelihoods, homes, and communities is an acceptable, though not a chargeable, cost of production. The washed-out farm and bankrupt farmer, the stripmined mountain and the unemployed or diseased miner, the clear-cut forest and the depressed logging town—all are seen as the mere natural results of so-called free enterprise. The pattern of industrial 'development' on the farm and in the forest, as in the coal fields, is that of combustion and exhaustion—not 'growth', a biological metaphor that is invariably contradicted by industrial practice.

The fault of a colonial economy is that it is dishonest: it misrepresents reality. In practice it is simply a way of keeping costs off the books of an exploitive interest. The exploitive interest is absent from the countryside exactly as if the countryside were a foreign colony. The result of this separation is that the true costs of production are not paid by the exploitive interest but only suffered by the exploited land and people. The colony, whether foreign or domestic, becomes unstable, both as an ecosystem and as a community because colonialism does not permit the development of strong local economies. The economy of a colony exports only 'raw material' and imports only finished goods. It buys and sells on markets over which it has no control; thus, both markets drain value from the colony. The economy of a colony is thus as far as possible from E.F.Schumacher's just (and safe) ideal of 'local production from local resources for local use'.

The way that a national economy preys on its internal colonies is by the destruction of community—that is, by the destruction of the principle of local self-sufficiency not only in the local economy but also in the local culture. Thus, local life becomes the dependent, and the victim, not just of the food industry, the transportation industry, the power industries, the various agribusiness industries, and so on, but also of the entertainment and the education and the religion industries—all involving change from goods once cheap or free to expensive goods having to be bought.

That the economy of most of rural America is a colonial economy became plain as soon as the local economies of subsistence lapsed and were replaced by the so-called 'consumer economy'. The old local economies of subsistence, which in America were often incomplete and imperfect, were nevertheless sources of local strength and independence, and, as I have suggested, they were a beginning on which we could have built. Their replacement by the 'consumer economy' has brought a helpless dependence on distant markets, on transported manufactured goods, on cash, and on credit.

Even so cursory a description of one of the old local subsistence economies as I gave at the beginning of this essay reveals that its economic assets were to a considerable extent intangible: culture-borne knowledge, attitudes, and skills; family and community coherence; family and community labour; and cultural or religious principles such as respect for gifts (natural or divine), humility, fidelity, charity, and neighbourliness. Such economies, furthermore, were mainly sun-powered, using plants and the bodies of animals and humans as 'solar converters'. By means of neighbourhood, knowledge, and skill, they were turning free supplies to economic advantage. Theirs was an economy that took place, largely, off the books. The wonderful fact, then, is that those emotional and spiritual values that are now so inconsequentially associated with the idea of community were economic assets in the old communities, and they produced economic results.

This finding can be corroborated by an example that is contemporary, though somewhat more removed from my own acquaintance and culture. David Kline and his family, who are members of one of the Amish communities in the hilly country of eastern Ohio, have a farm of 123 acres that, even in the present hard times, is successful, both economically and agriculturally. It is one of the farms that, in my thinking about agriculture, I have used as a standard.

Of the Klines' 123 acres, seventy-five are arable, twenty-nine are in permanent pasture, ten are forested, five are in orchard and gardens, and four are occupied by buildings. The major money-making enterprises of the farm are a dairy of twenty-three Guernsey cows (with about an equal number of heifers), and seven brood sows and a boar. The field crops, raised mainly to be fed on the place, are hay, corn, oats, and wheat. There are also the orchard and gardens, fifty laying hens, fifty pullets, fifty roosters for the table, and seven hives of bees. The farm combines commercial and subsistence enterprises, and its subsistence or household economy is obviously strong, producing some marketable surplus. In addition to the family's subsistence, this farm has been grossing about $50,000 a year, and netting $25,000 to $30,000. In 1985, the gross was $47,000, and the net $25,000. In the midst of an agricultural depression, this is a startling accomplishment. Again, it is an economic result that is only somewhat computable; it is accounted for also by the religious, cultural, family, and community coherence that is still maintained by the Old Order Amish, whose way of life, including their technology, makes possible the maximum utilization of natural (and therefore cheap or free) energy and fertility. A *full* accounting of David and Elsie Kline's economy would have to consider, as well, the extensive subsitutions of natural and cultural gifts for purchased supplies.

That David Kline is also an excellent conservationist and a naturalist, who may delay a hay-cutting in order to allow bobolink fledglings to leave the nest, makes him even more useful to us as an example. For a part of the Amish understanding of good work, built into their technology and their methods, is this respect for nature. Farming, to the Klines, is the proper husbanding of nature, a stewardly care for the natural integrities and processes that precede and support the life of the farm.

David once attended a conference on the subject of community. What is community, the conferees were asking, and how can we have it? At some point, late in the proceedings, they asked David what community was and what it meant to him. He said that when he and his son were ploughing in the spring he could look around him and see seventeen teams at work on the neighbouring farms. He knew those teams and the men driving them, and he knew that if he were hurt or sick, those men and those teams would be at work on his farm.

Conditioned as we all are now by industrial assumptions, we must be careful not to miss or to underestimate the point of David's reply: it is a practical description of a spiritual condition. With the Amish, economy is not merely a function of community; the community and the economy are virtually the same. We might, indeed, call an Amish community a loving economy, for it is based on the love of neighbours, of creatures, and of places. The community accomplishes the productive work that is necessary to any economy; the economy supports and preserves the land and the people. The economy cannot prey on the community because it is not alienated from the community; it *is* the community. We should notice too that David has described the economic helpfulness, the charity, that is natural to the life of a community—and free to members—that has been replaced, among most of the rest of us, by the insurance industry.

But let us go a little further and speculate on the relation between a subsistence-based family economy, such as the Klines' and a local—say, a county—economy. It is easy to assume, as I have said, that a subsistence-based family economy would be bad for the larger economy of the locality or county. But let us put beside the Kline farm an industrial Ohio farm of 640 acres (or one square mile), and let us say that this farm grosses $200,000 and nets $20,000. (I think that those are safe figures for our purpose, for midwestern industrial farmers have often found it impossible to net ten per cent of gross.) This square mile of land is *one* farm, farmed by *one* family, and therefore dependent on large-scale equipment. For years, as the people have been leaving the farms and the farms have been getting larger, the suppliers and servicers of farm machines, which have also been getting larger, have been withdrawing toward the larger towns. Now industrial farmers must sometimes drive astonishing distances for parts and repairs. For the farmer of a large industrial farm, the economic centre has thus moved far beyond the local community, and we must suppose that a large percentage of his operating costs goes outside the local community.

But a square mile of even reasonably good land would contain five farms more or less the size of the Klines'. If we suppose that the families would average three children each, this would increase the human population of the square mile from five to twenty-five. Such an increase in population implies a reduction in the scale of equipment, which in turn implies an increase of business for local suppliers and mechanics. Moreover, the population increase implies an increase of business for local shops and businesses of all kinds. If we use the Klines' farm economy as a base and suppose that the five farms average $50,000 a year gross and $25,000 a year net, then we see that they increase the gross income of the square mile by only $50,000. But individually, the five farms each would net $5,000 a year more than the large farm, and together they would increase the net income on the square mile to $125,000, an increase of net over the large single farm of $105,000.

This comparison is not entirely speculative; Marty Strange says, for instance, that in Iowa, in the years 1976 – 1983, small farms achieved '*more* output per dollar invested' than large farms. 'In fact,' he says, 'the larger the farm, the lower the output per dollar invested.' However, since my comparison must be at least partly speculative, I can hope only to suggest a possibility that has been ignored: that strong communities imply strong local economies, and vice versa—that, indeed, strong communities and strong local economies are identical.

Does this mean that, as local economies grow strong, there must be a concomitant weakening of the national economy? I do not think so. Strong local economies everywhere would, it seems to me, inevitably add up to strong national economies and to a strong world economy. The necessary distinction here is between temporary and permanent economic strength. A national economy may burgeon at the expense of its local economies, as ours has been doing, but, obviously, it can do so only for a while. The permanence of a national economy, we may be sure, would not be measurable by 'gross national product', which may, after all, involve local net deficits of, say, topsoil or underground water. It would have to be measured by the health of its communities, both human and natural.

If these communities are given no standing in the computations, then all costs and benefits to and from the community are 'externalized', and a business may show a profit to everybody else's loss. The cost of community to each of its members is restraint, limitation of scale. Its benefits, within acceptance of that limitation, are the many helps, human and natural, material and otherwise, that a community makes freely or cheaply available to its members. If an appropriate limitation of scale is not accepted, then the community is simply replaced by large-scale operators who work in isolation and by the dispossessed and excluded poor, who do not stay in place but drift into the cities where they are counted, no longer as 'surplus' farmers (or miners or woods workers) but as 'unemployed'.

If the human and natural communities are given no standing in the computations, then the large farm or other large enterprise acts as a siphon to drain economic and other values out of the locality into the 'gross national product'. This happens because its technology functions on behalf of the national economy, not the local community.

The bait that has opened communities to exploitation and destruction has always been ready cash for local people. But there has never been as much cash forthcoming to the local people as to people elsewhere—not by far. The supply of ready cash has tended to be undependable or temporary, and it has usually come as a substitute for things more permanent and dearer than cash, and harder to replace, once lost.

The only preventive and the only remedy is for the people to choose one another and their place over the rewards offered them by outside investors. The local community must understand itself finally as a community of interest—a common dependence on a common life and a common ground. And because a community is, by definition, *placed,* its success cannot be divided from the success of its place, its natural setting and surroundings: its soils, forests, grasslands, plants and animals, water, light and air. The two economies, the natural and the human, support each other. Each is the other's hope of a durable and a livable life.

Printed letterpress by Glenn Storhaug at Five Seasons Press, Madley, Hereford, from relief plates using Jan Tschichold's Sabon typeface photoset at Glevum Graphics in Gloucester. The preliminary pages and covers have been handset in Sabon and Garamond. The text is printed on *Five Seasons 100 per cent recycled book paper* made by William Sommerville and Son plc in Scotland.